101 Leadership Actions

for

Managing Change
in the 21st Century

OLLIE MALONE, JR., PH.D., D. MIN.

HRD Press • Amherst • Massachusetts

Published by: HRD Press
            22 Amherst Road
            Amherst, MA 01002
            800-822-2801 (U.S. and Canada)
            413-253-3488
            413-253-3490 (fax)
            www.hrdpress.com

ISBN 978-1-59996-226-9

Cover design by Eileen Klockars
Editorial services by Robert W. Carkhuff
Production services by Jean S. Miller

Dedication

This book is dedicated to the companies, individuals, teams, and systems that have contributed to my understanding of change management and have provided me with a context, dialogue, and a laboratory in which that understanding could be enhanced.

This book is also dedicated to my grand-daughters: Isabelle, Olivia, and Ava, who will be change agents in their generation.

Introduction

Any student of life and work in the twentieth century will recognize that life and work have changed in the twenty-first century.

One can focus on technology and the iPodization of a new generation, the microscopic footprints that our laptop computers now hold, or the fact that more information is accessible through the average cell phone than was previously accessible in a mainframe computer. Technology has changed—dramatically so—and it continues to do so.

But the changes are not restricted to technology. People have also changed in the shift from the twentieth to the twenty-first century. There are more women within the working population, more dual-career couples, more people of color, more people working beyond 65, and more people willing to say "Take this job and shove it." The people dimension, like the technology dimension, has changed dramatically.

Globalization, as well, has changed. Concerns about how management decisions in the United States will impact individuals across the globe are now quite common—despite the fact that a few decades ago we would not have been able to find the countries of concern to us on a map!

All of these concerns and changes have significantly impacted a leader's ability to lead the people, systems, and organizational structures for which he or she may be accountable. And there is little, if any, evidence that these factors driving change are slowing down. Every indicator suggests that they will continue to be significant factors that leaders cannot ignore as they develop and implement future strategies and initiatives.

This book is written to offer a perspective that has been shaped and informed by more than 30 years of leading and managing change in and with some of the largest corporations in America. This book does not pretend to have all of the answers to managing change—change is far too complex for that. It does, however, offer up proven ideas and perspectives that should be useful to the leader when considering his or her approach to change.

Whether the change is small in nature, or if it is so large that it will redefine the way work is done within your industry, the insights here should prove useful. These actions have been weighed, considered, and evaluated for their usefulness. Now they are presented to you with every hope that they will help make you rich and famous—and that you'll feel obliged to share the wealth with us.

To your success.

Ollie Malone, Jr., Ph.D.

Table of Contents

Prologue:
How to Read This Book

This book is not to be read like *Gone With the Wind* or *The Last of the Mohicans.* It's not that kind of book. This book is written for individuals who want to do something with the information they have obtained. Ideally, they will want to manage themselves, their teams, and the organizations in which they work in navigating the uncertain waters of change.

This being the case, there are several approaches one might use in reading this book:

- You can read the book as though everything listed in the book occurs within the order it is written. An attempt was made to write this book in a logical fashion, starting with you, the initiator of change, and concluding with considerations for creating a change-resilient organization. This change resiliency, we have found, is a critical point-of-view, considering the fact that within most organizations the changes are non-stop.

- You could also read this book by focusing on the chapters or suggestions in the book that seem most relevant to the change that you're facing. This functional view is useful and, if you are in a hurry, is not a bad way to get practical, timely information for the changes you are facing.

- You might also start with the first chapter (strongly recommended) then follow with whatever chapter strikes your fancy. This rather nomadic approach might capture your interest longer, since you're focusing only on those areas that are of interest to you—regardless of their practical benefit.

- Another alternative is for you to read this book in a community of leaders where you can compare notes, raise questions, and/or conduct a more robust dialogue about the ideas captured here. These leaders might be peers, direct reports, or individuals with whom you have a mentoring relationship. The most important criteria for those engaging in this dialogue, obviously, is that they are actively involved in creating change in their environments. Holding that primary criteria should ensure a relevant dialogue for all parties.

However you go about approaching the various chapters of this book, one recommendation is essential: read with the view of doing. The books in the 101 Leadership Action series are not designed for people who think about leadership; they are designed for individuals who do leadership—and who would like to do leadership better.

Now, let's get started.

Chapter 1
Change Starts at Home: Manage Yourself

In this chapter, we'll explore the critical role the leader plays in leading the change effort. A few decades ago, little attention was given to the importance of the leader initiating change in the change process. It was as if everything the leader did was fine and that the people just need to be "whipped into shape."

Not so.

Much of the information that has become available about failed efforts has pointed to the leader as an essential variable in successfully managing change. Whether the focus was on the leader managing his or her ego, managing his or her fears, or managing his or her resistance to the change he or she must lead, the leader is a critical variable, and to miss this essential reality is to doom your change (and yourself) to less than optimal results.

Conversely, by starting with yourself you can potentially accomplish a few goals:

1. You get to scrutinize yourself before (or as) others do. Too often the leader assumes that he or she is "on point" and that others are messed up (the "I'm OK, you're a disaster" posture), creating the type of arrogance and hubris that leaves the leader standing naked and ignorant.

2. You become your own diagnostician. Rather than waiting for someone else to point out opportunities for you to change in order to better align your leadership approach with the changes needed, you look carefully at your own approaches and identify the disconnects between what you have done and other approaches that may have been more effective.

3. You become, potentially, your own coach. External coaching is often a worthwhile investment in a leader's growth, but internal coaching is the ultimate goal of any coaching process. Internally scrutinizing your thoughts, your actions, and your interactions positions you to identify other alternatives that might be available to you. The combination of diagnosing and recommending alternatives should enable you to create great leadership-related questions that should begin a search for good leadership-related answers.

4. If you are a leader of leaders, you create a living example of how high-performing leaders self-manage and become self-reinforcing and, ultimately, self-sufficient leaders. You get to not only talk about how this is done, but you get to demonstrate the process.

5. You get to accelerate the pace of change far more rapidly, since you have dealt with yourself as a potential impediment to change. Having gotten yourself out of the way, you are no longer an impediment; you can now focus on others.

1 Commit to Managing Yourself

You may never have been all that interested in intense naval-gazing and that is not is being recommended at this stage.

But, let's face it: within your group, you are the filter. You filter what comes into your group and you filter what goes out of your group. You filter the messages, you filter the metrics, you shape the reality that is known within the group that you lead, and about your group to the leaders to whom you report.

Determine that before you take on any significant agenda, or any major transformative work, that you'll include yourself in the transformation. This is not to suggest that you must be at 100% before you can give attention to the rest of your agenda—if that were the case, no one would ever get started—but it does suggest that you will have to give attention to and commit to managing your own "stuff" while you help others manage theirs.

The other actions in this chapter are designed to make you more adept at managing your stuff. You don't have to do them all, but pick two or three particularly important ones that will help to define the leader you would want your direct reports and colleagues to see.

Let the change begin with you.

2 Take a Stroll Down "Memory Lane"

If you're like most leaders, you've been through a number of organizational and personal changes. It may have been something as seemingly insignificant as moving your office from one side of the building to another, or it may have been a divestiture of a company with a million employees—of which you were one.

Or, on a personal level, you may have gotten married, gotten divorced, had a child, or seen a child move across the country for his or her first professional employment. Whatever the catalyst, you've undoubtedly seen some changes in your day.

What were the best changes? Think of defining "best" as those changes that went most smoothly, where, despite the difficulty of the change, you and/or the others involved were able to navigate the change, focus on the essential tasks that needed to be accomplished, and come out on the other side of the change in a good place.

Think about those changes for a moment. As much as possible, try to stay with a change of recent note—one where the demands and complexities, as well as the resources and benefits of contemporary life, were present.

What made that change so good?

What would you want to take from that change into a change you might navigate in the future?

6

Now think about the other end of the change continuum—those changes that you hope no one will ever know you were involved with. Again, stay with contemporary examples and think about those realities that made these changes difficult, impossible, or ultimately embarrassing.

What made these changes a disaster?

What would you want to be sure to avoid from these previous changes?

3 Create Your STAR Criteria

Based on your review of the changes that went extremely well, as well as those changes that went poorly, select those high-priority items that you would say need to be included in your behavior going forward. Narrow this list down to the five to seven most important criteria that will define your success as a leader of a change initiative.

Consider the items you have just identified as your **S**ignificant **T**asks **A**nd **R**esults (STAR). These will define the targets for which you'll be shooting as you go through the change process.

Remember: Limit your STAR to a maximum of five to seven factors.

4 Audit Your STAR Performance

Having determined the most important behaviors for you, the leader of change, the question is (with apologies to Dr. Phil): "How's that working for you?" You may be excellent in the areas you've identified, or you may need a significant amount of work.

Create a scale, say, 1 to 5, or 1 to 10, then evaluate yourself on each of the STAR criteria you've identified.

The most important part of this audit is telling yourself the truth. Since you are providing your own assessment, you can obviously deceive yourself into believing you are far more adept at the STAR criteria than you really are, but what would be the point of that? You will live with the outcomes—whether fact or fiction.

Make it easy on yourself: tell the truth.

5 | Ask Others to Audit Your STAR Performance

One of the benefits of asking others to provide you with feedback is the opportunity you will get to see yourself through their eyes. Whether good or bad, you will have the ability to see yourself using the same criteria on which you've already evaluated yourself.

When asking others for their perspectives on how you go about managing change, get a wide range of opinions from those who have either seen or interacted with you in the process of creating change.

Whether you gather this information by anonymous survey (which we have found produces the most honest results), or if you use some other means of gathering the data, do it.

6 Determine the Critical Focus for Your Leadership Efforts

The combination of your observations and the observations of others should put you in a position to have a reasonably accurate assessment of your leadership competencies. With this information, you can gain an accurate perception of the areas that will enable you navigate the change.

Choose these areas relatively quickly. The goal is not to make perfect choices, but to make logical choices that allow you to get started.

Having started, you can always modify your goals and direction; once again, it is most important that you have a goal and a direction rather than having the perfect plan and direction. This is one time when 85% accuracy will serve you just fine.

7 Actively Learn from Other Change Leaders

For many leaders, the opportunity to get started in their change efforts seems equivalent to moving into a cave—separated from anyone else who may be undertaking a similar endeavor. Yet, the opportunity to compare notes, approaches, victories and defeats with others who are going through a similar process could prove to be of great value.

Capitalize on this.

Find those leaders in your department, division, state, or time zone with whom you can compare notes for mutual benefit.

Change is no longer a solo act. What you learn from your peers could revolutionize your approach to change and the ultimate value you derive from change.

Read articles and books, watch movies, and see change leaders in action. It will broaden the possibilities for action available to you.

Don't miss out.

8 Understand Your Resistance to Change

Although the topic of "resistance to change" is most often reserved for others' behavior, the leader can be guilty of manufacturing his or her own resistance. This resistance may be based on the nature of the change itself (you think it's just a dumb idea), the leader who initiated the idea (you think he or she is dumb), or it could be based on the timeframe and/or resources involved (How in the world can we be expected to do that much with that little in the timeframe presented?).

So where do you get stuck in your management of change? What is the catalyst that makes you want to "close up shop" and go do something else? Given your experience with change management, you have undoubtedly found yourself digging your heels in at various points. What prompted this?

As you and your group move forward, pay attention to these resistances. They could be your undoing.

9 Understand Others' Resistance to Change

The Myers-Briggs Type Indicator®, well-known among those who study human behavior, identifies 16 different personality types present in human populations. Assuming this is true, there are at least 15 viewpoints of change that may differ from your own.

For that reason, every leader entering into a change initiative should expect some level of resistance. The resistance may be based on a number of factors including:

- The timing of the change;
- The impact of the change;
- The inconvenience of the change;
- The players involved in the change (those who are leading the change);
- The beneficiaries of the change (those who will be better off as a result of the anticipated changes);
- The perceived "losers" in the change transaction.

These factors and others have the potential of influencing the popularity of the proposed change initiative, and often these perspectives have individuals' faces and backgrounds attached to them.

People do resist—often. Don't take that resistance personally.

10 Understand Your Resistance to Others' Resistance

For most individuals, when we have set out on a course we don't take kindly to interruptions, distractions, or other factors that will make the journey longer or that will potentially "mess up" our plans. Resistance often is seen this way.

The questions we get from others, their disagreements, the system issues that stand in the way and the numerous other "issues" have a way of creating irritants. And these irritants, true to their names, irritate.

It is possible, then, for others' resistance to create further resistance for you, the leader.

Recognize when this "dance of resistance" is about to begin. If you can recognize it and manage it, you are well on your way to unhooking yourself from its disastrous consequences.

11 Engage the Resistance Responsibly

The fact is, in many organizations resistance creates a bit of a dance between the parties—whether it involves the leader and the led, the led with the led, or some other mixture of the players. Resistance has a way of creating its own drama that is often like a second (or third) ring in a three-ring circus.

Although resistance can create a life of its own, you, the leader, have some choice of strategies with regard to what you're going to do with the resistance that emerges. You can:

A. Engage it and wrestle it to the ground;

B. Ignore it and hope that it will go away;

C. Negotiate with it (If I do this, will you do this?);

D. Delegate it to someone else and hope that they have a clue as to how to deal with it;

E. Manage it quickly, respectfully, and, where appropriate, investigate it further to extract the value or merit from it.

Of the five strategies indicated, our experiences have found that "E" provides the best long-term strategy for dealing with resistance. It acknowledges the presence of the resistance, the validity (possibly) of the resistance, and it attempts to leverage the value of the resistance for improving processes, relationships, information, or ultimate outcomes.

12 Keep Yourself in View

The demands of change are great, and for those who are identified as change leaders the demands are often greater still. Within the process of managing change, it becomes quite easy for the change leader to lose sight of him- or herself.

The leader's usual routine is often at risk during change. This routine might include exercise, eating right, spending time with friends and family, and engaging in a form of self-renewal (thinking about the work he or she is doing, planning ahead, learning new approaches), as well as getting adequate rest.

Because these are the practices that energize the leader and keep him or her buoyant, it is important that the leader maintain these to the degree possible. The demands of the change may suggest that the leader cannot do all of his or her usual "routine," but it is advantageous if the leader can hold on to some sense of normalcy during the change. This routine provides a sense of the familiar during times of change—and when everything else may be up for grabs, it is highly useful for the leader to have something that feels like "home."

13 Know That You'll See This Movie Again

One of the most critical shifts in change management from the 20th century to the 21st century lies in the frequency with which change is being managed. Those who were born, grew up, married, began a career, retired from that career, and attended the same place of worship for 50 years might have a challenge with the pace and the frequency with which change is now being managed.

But it is here.

Just ask those individuals who suffered one natural disaster only to find that another natural disaster, perhaps even more devastating, was on its heels. In some respects, what we see reflected in weather patterns is equally relevant to our organizations. Ask the folks at AT&T, or Enron, or GM, or Toyota, or any number of other organizations who, despite having navigated previous changes, have taken on new challenges.

To whatever degree you convey a message that suggests that the organization will soon be "back to normal," you participate in deceiving those who work for you. That which has historically been occasional change is now constant change.

As a leader, set that expectation. You and your team will be living with variations on this reality.

Parting thoughts...

In a time of drastic change, it is the learners who inherit the future. The learned usually find themselves equipped to live in a world that no longer exists.

– Eric Hoffer

The great achievers, a Napoleon, a Leonardo da Vinci, a Mozart, have always managed themselves. This in large measure made them great achievers. But they were the rarest of exceptions. And they were so unusual, both in their talents and in their achievements, as to be considered outside the boundaries of normal human existence. Now even people of modest endowments, that is, average mediocrities, will have to learn to manage themselves.

– Peter Drucker
Management Challenges for the 21st Century

Chapter 2
Lead Others

Few human events underscore the need for leadership in the way change does. Whether the change is a natural disaster, an unexpected event, or the well-planned execution of a well-known change, leadership is required.

If you are in a leadership role, that leadership is you. You are the one to whom direct reports look for answers and bosses look for well-executed implementation. You are the one with whom the buck stops and who may be accountable for some small or large part of the ultimate outcome of the change.

And you are also the one who must align others in order for the change to happen. Whether in large part or in small part, your ability to get individuals focused, engaged, and marching forth will determine the degree to which your change leadership efforts are wildly successful or an unmitigated disaster.

In this chapter focusing on "Leading Others" we'll explore:

- Creating and utilizing a well-honed vision;

- Leveraging technology to create a plan worth executing;

- Assigning roles and responsibilities for the change;

- Establishing clear standards for the work to be accomplished;
- Cultivating a climate conducive to doing good work.

Within each of these areas, you'll be provided with a number of suggestions that will enable you to lead others well.

14 Cast the Vision— Meaning #1

The term "cast" is useful in multiple manner in relation to the leader's use of vision.

In thinking as an artist would think, the vision is the product of the mind of the creator. As an organizational leader, you have the opportunity of creating a vision that is useful to yourself and to others in creating optimal change results. Like the artist, the leader has the opportunity to create, or cast, the vision. Unlike some artists' work, the vision should not be cast in stone. It is ideal that the vision be cast allowing it to flex to meet the dynamic demands of the environment.

15 Cast the Vision— Meaning #2

Thinking as a physician, the vision may need to be kept in a cast; that is, shielded and protected until its essential parts can come together well and help support the organizational strength needed during times of change.

While demands of the change could require that change be implemented quickly, the possibility also exists that change can be implemented poorly or without sufficient forethought in terms of the impact of the change on those most affected by it.

This action argues for good timing—and not presenting the vision until the timing aligns well with the opportunity.

16 Cast the Vision— Meaning #3

Much in the same way that a Hollywood director casts a team of actors to deliver top-notch performances in the director's work, the vision also requires casting.

Once the vision has been created, it may become clear that you lack the full complement of skills essential for the vision's fulfillment. Identify the deficiency and cast your vision for success with the team that has the capabilities and enthusiasm to achieve the desired results.

17 Ensure That Your Vision Includes Others

The term "line of sight" is extremely useful in the achievement of this action. Individuals need to see themselves in the vision you have created. Whether the work aligns perfectly with their roles and responsibilities, or whether the attitudes and convictions of the vision align with their personal attitudes and convictions, individuals need to see that they "fit in."

This may require a level of translation, since the majority of workers are not accustomed to being energized or directed by a vision.

18 Invite Others to Enlist in the Achievement of the Vision

If your vision for change is to achieve everything hoped for, it will require the active engagement and participation of others in its achievement. It will take far more than your energies alone to ensure its achievement.

So ask.

Too often individuals sit on the sidelines waiting to be invited into the game. Meanwhile, leaders are wondering why those sitting on the sidelines haven't gotten up and jumped into the game. It doesn't matter.

Ask them.

A simple, "Can I count on your active support in helping make this vision a reality?" may get the job done, or you may have to identify some other means of enlistment, but without a specific enlistment process the leader will be left to wonder whether the individual is "in" or "out."

Don't guess. Ask.

19 Encourage Others to Own the Vision

There is a critical difference between driving a car and owning a car. When an individual drives a car, there is the obligatory attention to traffic signs, to pedestrians, and to the rules of the road.

When the same individual owns a car, he or she maintains it, protects it from premature destruction, and wards off those elements that would diminish its value.

So it is with the vision. The vision needs to be owned, and the ultimate aim of the vision will come much more closely in view when the ownership of the vision expands beyond its creator.

Sell the vision—and watch others take on the joys of ownership.

20 Create a Skeletal Plan

The vision alone does not ensure its achievement, any more than a picture of your desired destination ensures your accurate, timely, and safe arrival. Arriving at your desired destination will require translating the vision into a set of major achievements essential for the vision's completion.

21 Set Milestones for Significant Accomplishments

Once you have identified the major achievements, identify target dates for their completion. This task requires a well-reasoned specificity, where you can determine what needs to be done and where you can identify the date the desired efforts should be achieved.

Expecting people to know when results should be achieved, yet not being specific regarding the dates and the expected outcomes, is a recipe for disaster. Avoid that pothole; set milestones for the achievement of the goals desired.

22 Create Supporting Technical Mechanisms for Plan Achievement

The availability today of project-related software virtually guarantees that no project ever need to be late or off-target. Even most simple calendar software allows you to enter information that could be useful in planning a project or ushering the project through to completion.

Find the software that works well for you.

Fall in love with it.

Get that software to work for you.

23 Create Supporting Interpersonal Mechanisms for Plan Achievement with Those Above You

Change, even change that is technologically supported, shifts the leader's focus away from the people being led to any number of other things that emerge in the process. For that reason, leadership effectiveness requires that you create mechanisms or methods that create the kind of ongoing dynamic dialogue and exchange of ideas that is essential for the care and feeding of the vision and the plans that support its achievement.

Create brief updates for those above you that focus on:

- Where you're going (your vision);

- Where you are (your plan and milestones);

- Where things are working (your accomplishments);

- Where you need help or insight (their role and support).

These four items, reviewed on a regular basis with those whom you support, should ensure that you have the type of familiarity with those above you that will make your goals achievable.

24 Create Supporting Interpersonal Mechanisms for Plan Achievement for Those Beside You

Even though your peers aren't directly in your line of authority, keep them familiar with your work and the ways in which you can collaborate more effectively and in a manner that might be mutually supportive.

All too often, leaders take their change agendas and, like the family dog, bury them in the background (metaphorically, of course), making it impossible for others to even know about the goals and directions the leader may be pursuing—much less be able to contribute to the quality of the thinking or the actions.

Bring your vision and the plan to achieve it out in the open and welcome the input of those whose insight, knowledge and skill could be just the ticket to your ultimate success.

Create brief updates for those beside you that focus on:

- Where you're going (your vision);

- Where you are (your plan and milestones);

- Where things are working (your accomplishments);

- Where you need help or insight (their role and support).

25 Create Supporting Interpersonal Mechanisms for Plan Achievement for Those Below You

The challenge of getting things done in organizations often puts the leader in a position that allows one of the most important aspects of his or her work—leading people—undone. This is tragic.

This tragedy is often magnified because of the multiple demands, short timeframes, and the urgency of the outcomes and results.

It is precisely for these reasons (multiple demands, short timeframes, and urgency of outcomes) that staying in touch with one's direct reports becomes even more critical. This doesn't require multi-day conferences, but it does require a commitment to being open and informative and to engaging in exchanges that could prove mutually-beneficial.

Create brief updates for those below you that focus on:

- Where you're going (your vision);

- Where you are (your plan and milestones);

- Where things are working (your accomplishments);

- Where you need help or insight (their role and support).

26 Create Supporting Interpersonal Mechanisms for Plan Achievement for Those Diagonal to You

There are others in your organization, as well, who may not be in your direct line of authority. These individuals likely fall into a category of "stakeholders" that could include customers or members of other departments with whom you partner.

Keeping these individuals informed is also an important dimension of your leadership. This does not suggest that you spend equivalent amounts of time with individuals in these departments or functions, but their involvement in the success of your plan cannot be discounted.

Like the others discussed, these individuals need to engage with you periodically in order to know:

- Where you're going (your vision);

- Where you are (your plan and milestones);

- Where things are working (your accomplishments);

- Where you need help or insight (their role and support).

27 Accept No Idle Players

The achievement of organizational change demands the full participation of all those individuals within the organization. Whether they are directly involved in the achievement or only play a small role, their familiarity with the direction and purpose of the change, as well as their understanding of their role, is extremely important to the ultimate success of the change effort.

Whether an individual has a clearly-defined role or not, he or she should be actively engaged in the process. In fact, they should be actively engaged in some aspect of the change until they (and you) have clarified the role and expected outcomes from their efforts.

Incorporate this "no idle player" policy in your regular communications with those who work with you.

28 Review Individual Accountabilities

Once people are in motion (Action 27), it is easier to shape and refine the direction that they take. Getting them going from a dead start is often a seemingly-impossible task.

In reviewing and reestablishing individual accountabilities, individuals should be well aware of:

- Where their work comes from (how they fit in the flow of work);

- What are the primary duties they are accountable for;

- What excellence looks like in their area(s) of responsibility;

- The recipient of their work and what that recipient needs from this individual in order to perform his or her work well.

29 Update Individual Accountabilities

Keeping individuals focused is one of the primary tasks of a well-executed change process. By doing so, you will ensure that individuals are bringing value to the change and are keeping themselves sufficiently focused to avoid the distractions of things that either can't be addressed, won't be addressed during the current timeframe, or those things that require the input and regulation of others to accomplish.

There are few things more frustrating to individuals than finding out that the things on which they have worked for some extended period of time are no longer relevant to the work going forward.

Rather than running the risk of this rude reality, ensure that individuals' accountabilities are up-to-date and reflect the current thinking about the work that needs to be done.

30 Jointly and Aggressively Set WIGS and WAGS

What should be the focus of individuals' energies for a given time period? How can you and the individual structure those responsibilities in such a way that they are challenging, relevant, meaningful, and high-impact?

Rather than taking this task on as exclusively yours, make sure your direct reports understand the importance of bringing their own expertise, insights, and analysis to this conversation. Frankly, this is what brings the ultimate value to their contribution to the organization. If their only role is to sit and wait for instruction, they are likely paid far more than is appropriate.

The combination of the individual's expertise with your knowledge should enable you to produce both WIGS (Wildly Important Goals) and WAGS (Wildly Aggressive Goals).

31 Jointly and Aggressively Set WIGS and WAGS

Before individuals can act on the good, the bad, and the ugly, they must understand what it is— what it looks like, what contributes to its good- ness, badness, or ugliness and how their efforts can contribute to a better outcome.

Generate as accurate a picture of the ideal results as possible. For most individuals, this will make the process of achieving the desired results far more possible and quicker.

Parting thoughts...

Never tell people how to do things. Tell them what to do and they will surprise you with their ingenuity.

– Gen. George S. Patton

All of the great leaders have had one characteristic in common: it was the willingness to confront unequivocally the major anxiety of their people in their time. This, and not much else, is the essence of leadership.

– John Kenneth Galbraith

The future is not a result of choices among alternative paths offered by the present, but a place that is created—created first in the mind and will, created next in activity. The future is not some place we are going to, but one we are creating. The paths are not to be found, but made, and the activity of making them, changes both the maker and the destination.

– John Schaar

Chapter 3
Prepare Early

Before anything else, preparation is the key to success.

– Alexander Graham Bell

The business of organizational change wrecks havoc on all parties involved. The focus of individuals' work changes, relationships change, customer demands change—it all seems up for grabs. Those who have ordered their lives and work like clockwork are left feeling disoriented, disheveled, and "dissed" in general.

Since a significant part of the leader's success is based on his or her ability to maintain the organization's results during times of change, preparation— mentally and otherwise—becomes critical. There is no substitute for good preparation, and there are few antidotes for poor preparation.

As you become mentally prepared and share that preparation with others, they are able to anticipate the demands of a rapidly changing reality. As a result, the organization will be better able to anticipate the change and, when it arrives, better able to navigate the rapids of change.

32 Know Your Industry

Whether your industry is pharmaceuticals or financial reporting, it carries with it certain skills, knowledge, realities, and disciplines that are subject to change. Historically, the more you know about the industry, the more you are able to track the patterns of your industry and the better able you are to anticipate the changes that may occur in your industry.

Track your "industry"—whether that industry is your company, your professional field or your city. Know that entity and how it operates. This will provide you with a means of anticipating changes and preparing well for them.

33 Watch Your Industry Patterns

Where is your industry going? What are the implications of this direction for you and your organization? An example might prove to be useful:

> When technology became sufficiently sophisticated to provide training to individuals at their desks (rather than requiring them to attend training in a classroom), it became obvious to one training manager that he would no longer need a training staff the size that he had. In relatively short order, he determined that he would: 1) not backfill available openings for training staff; 2) move several members of his in-class training team into the online training function; and 3) ramp up the distance learning part of his training function.

As you are able to see where your industry is going, you can get ahead of the curve on the needed changes.

34 Train Your Staff to Observe the Trends

In addition to your own observation of the trends, your staff needs to be likewise informed and ready to tackle the changes as they emerge.

Insist that your staff knows what's happening in the company or what may be happening in the industry.

35 Join a Professional Community

Virtually every professional discipline has its own professional community or association. These associations serve several purposes: they provide networking opportunities for their members; they keep their members informed as to changes in their field and the implications of those changes for the members' work; and they also provide an environment where members can learn and grow in their respective disciplines.

In terms of change, these groups often have their fingers on the pulse of the organizations that influence the future of the field. They are largely aware of the stakeholders of the field and where these stakeholders are setting their sights next.

As you interact with a professional community, you can better anticipate the changes that are coming in the industry.

36 Actively Address Industry Trends

Staff meetings, one-on-one conversations, and small group chats all provide opportunities to explore where the company, your professional discipline, or the community in which you operate may be heading.

All of these entities have implications for you and your team, as well as your collective work. The significance of these implications is often lost, however, if the topics are not brought to the forefront of discussions.

Talk about these trends. Make sure your team members can connect the dots between the present and the future. As you are able to do so, you shorten the transition period from what is currently done and what may need to be done in the future.

37 Play "What If" Games

"What if" games, if played well and regularly, provide mental and intellectual exercise for your team.

Playing "what if" games simply requires you to think of a condition and explore the possibilities that might occur as a result of that condition. For example, "What if we were no longer able to meet with clients face-to-face? How could we do our jobs effectively under those circumstances?"

These "what if" games are also the beginning of scenario planning, which could also be a useful exercise in anticipating the future.

38 Build Full-Fledged Scenarios

As was indicated in the previous action, scenario planning can be a useful exercise for those anticipating change. It can also be a useful exercise for those who are not anticipating change, because it develops the group's thinking beyond the present and into possibilities for the future.

Scenarios can be quite complex or they can be simplistic. Whatever approach you take to the building of these scenarios, recognize them for the learning potential that is in them.

And, to the degree that your group is actively involved in creating scenarios, it is actively looking at the future and subconsciously planning for it.

39 Create an Established Approach to Change

In many respects, approaches to change are much like diets; there are many of them, and many of them work. The issue, then, is not finding the one "silver bullet" of change, but finding a change process to which you are willing to commit and one that you are willing to see through.

And after you have identified this approach to change, ensure that it is well-known among the individuals in your organization. This will speed up the process of change, because the roadmap for change will be clear for all of the participants.

40 Train Your Team on Your Established Approach to Change

Although there are many reasons that changes in organizations are less than successful, one reason lies in the fact that there are multiple approaches to change, each of which requires translation before the work of change begins.

If there is a dominant approach to change in your organization, make sure all of your team members are familiar with that approach and utilize it. It will increase the depth of the dialogue among members of the team, as well as the ability to navigate the change far more quickly.

41 Apply Your Approach to Change to Small, Insignificant Changes

The old sales adage, "Try before you buy," seems to be appropriate here. Before you invite individuals to mortgage their personal and professional futures on a change process that they may have learned but never tried out, allow them to take the process out on a "test drive."

It's rather like learning to dance before the big dance; having ironed out the kinks, individuals are able to move forward with greater speed when speed becomes the central issue.

42 Capture Multi-Level Learning from Your Trial Run

Having completed a "trial run" on a project of lesser importance allows you and your team to capitalize on that experiment for future application. It's useful to explore:

- What you learned about yourself and your ability to manage change;

- What you learned about your team and its ability to manage change;

- What you learned about the organization's ability to manage change;

- What you may have learned about change management in general.

If the change process has been well-managed, you and your team will emerge with a head full of information about what you did, what worked well, and what you might want to do differently next time.

You'll be getting smarter.

43 Make Change the Norm

In too many organizations, and among too many individuals, change is the exception. Some organizations (and individuals) work diligently to avoid anything that looks like change—holding on to the familiar when a new approach would be far more beneficial.

Seek opportunities to develop the "change muscle" of your organization.

44 Identify the Change Leaders in Your Organization

Organizational change mastery requires the presence of individuals who cannot only navigate the change but help others to do so, as well. Their presence creates a built-in expertise useful to you as well as to others in the organization.

Who are those individuals in your organization?

Do you have a few? A lot? How many?

Make sure you know who they are and where they are located in the organization. Their influence could be quite useful to your change efforts—both present and future.

45 Increase the Capacity of Those Change Leaders

Ultimately, change management can best serve you and your organization when it is a well-ingrained competency both within your leadership role and in the roles of other individuals.

This being the case, look for opportunities to expand your understanding of change and its effectiveness, as well as the understanding of other change leaders in this important area.

46 Put "Change" on the Agenda

Formal meetings are a great way to underscore the things that are most important in your organization. Assuming you have regular staff meetings, periodic conferences, or other meetings where the important issues of your business are discussed, add "change" to that agenda.

This addition will allow for formal, systematic information to be shared about change and its impact on your organization. And it should dovetail with the ongoing dialogue focusing on change that occurs on a daily basis.

47 Talk About Change as the Norm

Make change and change management as normal a part of the conversation you have in your organization as organizational results, customer needs, and other key aspects of your overall success. Change management is an overall part of your skill set and needs to be managed as such—until further notice.

Change also needs to be a norm for those who work with you—whether they are other managers, direct reports, or colleagues in the organization.

Do your part: talk about the current changes and upcoming changes in the organization as if they were the norm. After all, they are.

Parting thoughts...

Good luck is the residue of preparation.

– Jack Youngblood

But to me the bottom line is the more education you can give yourself, and the more preparation you can do, the less chance of failing.

– Stuart Pearce

Chapter 4
Recognize Change as a Participative Sport

There are those sports that are best left to the professionals—bull riding, for example. As a sport, bull riding should not be undertaken by rank novices; the consequences are potentially disastrous.

Running, however, could be undertaken by anyone with a desire to join in. The risks are minimal, the likelihood of enjoyment is high, and the training required to enter is not overwhelming.

"Change," as a sport, is like running: just about anyone can participate in it, it requires some preparation although not a significant amount, and everyone can derive benefit by having participated.

In previous centuries, change was announced. The boss, by memo or by verbal indication, would signify the fact that a change was going to happen. Shortly thereafter, he or she would inform the workers of their respective roles in the change process.

The rapid, unrelenting pace of change in the twenty-first century has greatly truncated the process. An announcement is no longer necessary—staff can assume that change is ongoing and never ending. It may slow down, but it doesn't end. And the rapid pace of the current change says that an individual needs to assume that he or she has a role—and then get on with it.

In this chapter, we'll explore the actions that can help get your entire organization engaged in the process of change. We'll also explore those things that might stand in the way of broad participation—and how to address those issues.

48 Think Like an Olympic Coach—with No Athletes

As a change leader, you will craft a vision, engage and train others in seeing the vision come about, and manage a system that ensures that the results you receive are the results you desired. You're a big deal in the change process.

But your contribution to the change efforts will be severely compromised without the active and wholehearted engagement of key individuals in the organization.

Think like an Olympic coach who has the knowledge and skills to take home gold—and who just needs athletes to be trained and, ultimately, stand to receive the awards.

49 Sell a Personal Change

Every person joins the change effort based on some sense of enlightened self interest.

Help individuals discover their WII-FM (What's in it For Me?), so that change has some staying power to it. The change doesn't simply come because "the boss said so," but because the change is of some perceived value or opportunity for impact based on one's goals, vision, or values.

50 Listen as People Tune in to WII-FM

A behavioral science adage is that "people do those things that they perceive to be in their enlightened self interest." Change is no exception.

As individuals are engaged in the change process, their "hot buttons" will become clearer. What they're interested in will be clear, what they want to see happen will be clear, and what they don't want to see happen will also be clear.

51 Be a Good Marketer

Years ago, marketers told us that "perceptions define reality" and, indeed, they were right. Every day individuals come in to work with certain perceptions—about the work, about the boss, about the coworkers, about the tasks to be accomplished, about the customer, about the company—the list goes on and on.

Good marketers shape perceptions. They help individuals see those things that are in the best interest of the outcome that they would like to create. That's your task.

What are those things that individuals need to see, to know, to understand in order to get actively engaged in the change needed? Focus on those—and make sure individuals understand how they relate.

52 | Increase Active Participation in Change

It's not hard to find passive participants. They are everywhere. Just look at any baseball game that someone has described as "18 men desperately needing rest being watched by thousands of folks desperately needing exercise."

Encourage your team to get out of the stands. Their greatest value and contribution is when they are involved in change—not merely offering commentary on it.

53 Retire the Analysts

Any initiative generates analysts. You know them—they're the ones who sit on the sidelines and make endless comments. These comments, generally, are not terribly helpful, since they don't suggest what to do to resolve the issues; they only bemoan the current state.

In some respects, it is like Howard Cosell's book, *I Never Played the Game*: there are numerous individuals who believe themselves qualified to make ongoing commentary on how screwed up everything is, but have no skills to bring about change.

Do not allow this attitude to take root on your team. Retire the analysts before they push your team into early retirement.

54 Build Change All-Stars

Virtually every field of endeavor has its all-stars. There are basketball all-stars, baseball all-stars, musical all-stars; there are all-stars in every field. It's time change had its all-stars.

If change had its own set of all-stars, they would be individuals that are highly skilled in areas of change—so much so that they would be desired by others for their change competence. No doubt, you could use a few change all-stars in your organization.

The good news is you can grow them yourself—to your own specifications.

55 Cross-Train

One of the challenges of having a highly-competent staff is that they are constantly in demand—both inside and outside of the organization. It's not uncommon to find that the individual that you regard highly is also highly regarded by others. Sometimes the level of regard is so high that the individual may be hired away for more money and a greater opportunity than you can provide in your organization.

This is not an argument for leaving your employees clueless, rather it is an argument for building a cadre of individuals who can operate in a variety of positions within your organization. The greater the flexibility you have with your team members, the less likely you'll be rattled by the exiting of a key team member.

56 Stack Critical Skills Deeply

The current climate in most organizations creates a situation where the talent base is quite thin. "We're about one deep," one client recently said, "and we're praying he doesn't go anywhere."

Having only one individual in key areas of skill performance is risky business. If the individual becomes ill, gets a better offer, or wins the lottery, the organization is in a world of hurt.

Make sure the most important skill areas have multiple individuals who are capable of performing multiple critical tasks.

57 Build a Self-Coaching Team

Self-coaching teams are amazing. Not only do you have the benefit of high-performing players, but any one of these players, as needed, can step into a coaching role of offering wisdom, intuition, and strategic insight into the team's work.

This degree of flexible leadership ensures that whatever and whenever a crisis occurs, leadership will be present to bring clarity and direction to the work that needs to be done.

To the degree that you have a self-coaching team, you don't limit your team's effectiveness to your availability. Whether you are on site or not, leadership takes place and individuals are able to get important tasks done.

58 Give Your Injured Players a Role

I often find it amazing that when basketball players are injured, they do nothing. Despite the fact that they know the game, know the players, and may even know the opponent's name, they dress in suits and sit in the stands.

Maybe it's just me.

It would seem, however, that if an individual is being paid as well as these players are, there would be some role for them that could be useful to the team, despite the fact that they are unable to take on the primary role for which they were hired.

The roles may be small in nature—and may consist of cheering the team on, offering specific suggestions and insights to players who may be struggling, or ensuring that there is significant team spirit on the bench. Whatever the role, these players can do more than appear to sit and wait on a photo shoot for *GQ Magazine*.

Even though unforeseen circumstances can take your players out of their primary roles, make sure they stay connected to the team by taking on roles useful to the team. This enables them to stay connected to the team, and the team to stay connected to them.

59 Get Everyone Suited Up

In many sporting endeavors, "game day" requires that everyone gets dressed and ready to play. The coaches, the assistant coaches, the players, and the cheerleaders are all dressed.

Getting suited up is a part of the game.

How will you get your players suited up? It may require a change of wardrobe, but it may also require a change of attention. Suited up players in the sporting world have their attentions set on the game coming up. They're not distracted by other events or those events that may be tangential to the big game.

Get your players operating in the same way.

60 Succeed with a Positive Mental Attitude

Those who win want to win. Seldom do individuals or teams win who really don't want to win. They have prepared to win, they are focused on winning, and they operate in a manner that reflects that focus.

How about your team? Are they focused on winning—despite the challenges that may face them? Do they believe they can win? If they do, they are well on their way to performing well.

Tennis champion Jimmy Connors once said, "When you get to a certain level of tennis skill, 95% of whether you win or lose can be chalked up to your mental attitude."

If you have prepared your team with the skills they need to succeed, you must also prepare them with a mental attitude that accompanies these skills.

61 Monitor Mental Attitude Patterns on Your Team

Although most leaders have been trained to look for results, outcomes, and achievements, much of the research on organizational performance shows that the methodologies used to obtain results can be either helpful or harmful to the organization's ultimate results.

For this reason you, the leader, need to keep a sharp eye on the mental attitudes present in your team.

Many individuals have patterns of mental attitude. Some are great until difficulties come, then they fold like a cheap suit. Others, when facing difficulties, bear down, dig in, and get the job done.

Spend some time noticing them. Not every less-than-ideal attitude needs to be commented on, but it will be useful to comment on recurring patterns that create difficulties for the individuals or for the team with whom the individual works.

62 Coach for Emotional Intelligence

The research on organizational effectiveness reflects the fact that emotional intelligence (the ability to manage one's own emotions and to support others in managing their emotions) is a far greater measure of one's ultimate success than is IQ alone. In other words, you can be brilliant, but if you can't manage yourself or help others to manage themselves you will likely fall short of your potential.

You may have noticed this among your team members. Some individuals may be brilliant intellectually but socially and emotionally lacking.

The good news is that emotional intelligence can be learned. And if it can be learned, it can be coached.

And since it can be learned, you'll have the honor of coaching it.

Get started.

63 Measure Emotional Intelligence

Since the mental game is a critical part of any team's performance, measuring your team in this domain would serve you and the team members well.

When you measure your team's emotional intelligence, you will be better able to:

- Recognize your team's emotional strengths and weakness;

- Provide a baseline against which individuals can measure their emotional growth and effectiveness in the same way that they would measure other skill areas;

- Identify areas of social and emotional growth that will enable your team members to perform even better in the long-run.

64 Measure Your Own Emotional Intelligence

What's the use of having an emotionally intelligent team when you, the leader, may be lacking in critical areas?

Make sure you're setting not only an intellectual pace but also a developmental pace for individuals in your organization. As they see you grow, they will likely be more willing to take on the risk and challenge of growth for themselves.

As you're measuring the team's emotional intelligence, make sure your emotional intelligence is also being well-monitored.

65 Create a Game Plan to Develop Your Emotional Intelligence

While you are making sure that your team's emotional intelligence is strong, don't neglect your own.

As the leader, you set the pace. Your team members will likely take their clues from you; make sure you're not misfiring.

Including yourself in the measurement of emotional intelligence says to your team, "I'm in the game, too." It signals the fact that although you are the leader, you are also a learning leader—one who wants to get better at what he or she does.

Start working on your own emotional intelligence—you'll likely find individuals on your team who need to work on the same issues.

Parting thoughts...

The speed of the leader is the speed of the gang.

– Mary Kay Ash

A living thing is distinguished from a dead thing by the multiplicity of the changes at any moment taking place in it.

– Herbert Spencer

Throughout my career, I swam for form. Speed came as a result of it.

– Johnny Weissmuller

Chapter 5
Create a Change Army

Entire nations have been known to be moved by a well-trained army. And if an army can move a nation, an army will likewise be able to move your team, your division, group, or company.

You need a change army.

But getting an army is seldom easy. Armies demand hard work, dedication, self-sacrifice, and commitment to the welfare of others. They demand a greater level of dedication than does a team.

That's a tough sale, but it has been known to happen.

And for those who join the change army, the psychic rewards are unbelievable. The level of self-esteem one gains by having been a part of an army that has high standards, high demands, and high rewards is exceptional.

If the change that you and your organization seek is a great one, then you will need great women and men to step up to the challenge. If the challenge is mediocre, then a mediocre team will do. Increasingly, however, organizations are demanding higher and greater levels of change ("step change," "level change" and "system redesign" are not unfamiliar terms these days).

If you'll need a well-equipped army to bring about the change you desire, start now.

66 Understand the Depth of the Challenge

If building an army is important to your overall success, you must first understand the depth and the complexity of the challenge that is before you. How big? How wide? How long? How much? You must understand the weightiness of the challenge you're selling if you are going to be able to help understand the dimensions of the challenge.

If the challenge is not a great one, perhaps you don't need an army. If it is more "business as usual," then continue doing what you've been doing and you'll likely be in an adequate space.

But for many "business as usual" falls far short of what is needed for the change that is before you. You may have a "white sheet" challenge, where you're starting from scratch. That's not easy, but it can and has been done.

But you need a special team to do that.

67 Create Metaphors of What Is

For some, metaphors are for poets, i.e., "Thou art lovely as a summer day." Yet, even people from East Texas use metaphors: "She was so skinny she could hula hoop with a Cheerio." East Texans are not to be outdone.

Metaphors create a colorful picture between two entities and thereby enable a greater understanding of the one that may be least known. Metaphors are used in a variety of creative endeavors, and they can be used to manage change.

Create metaphors of what is. To what could you compare the current state of the organization? In working with one group, a group member described the organization as "a vacant lot, where the building had long since been torn down and the ground paved over. Only the birds come to visit the former facility—accompanied by a homeless woman, who, from her tattered clothes, feeds them bread crumbs."

68 Create Metaphors of What Is To Be

Just as metaphors can create powerful pictures of the current state, they can also be useful in creating pictures of the desired future state. Think of some powerful change agents and the metaphors they used:

Martin Luther King: *I have a dream*

Mother Teresa: *Ministering to the least and the lost*

FDR: *Two chickens in every pot*

Ford Motor: *Has a better idea*

Future-oriented metaphors have been known to engage individuals on the sidelines—often more quickly than the most eloquent of lengthy speeches. And they create powerful snapshots of what could be.

Put your brain to work and identify the types of metaphors that speak to the future you would want to see this change army create.

69 Compare the Past to the Future

Another powerful device used by skillful change agents is the use of comparisons. The use of comparisons not only presents a picture of the magnitude of change needed, but these comparisons often interject a level of humor in the conversation:

> *"In the past we were a Pinto; now I want us to be a Maserati."*

> *"We need to go from Alpo to high-po."*

Challenge your team through the use of language that provides a sense of the shift that is necessary from the present (or past) state to the future.

70 Draw Pictures

Visual images, even crudely drawn, are often useful in capturing the essence of change. Unfortunately for many leaders, performance orientation kicks in and individuals intimidate themselves with the idea of having to draw, rather than understanding that the purpose of the drawing is to capture their thoughts and feelings—not to create a jury-ready work.

As the old saying goes, "A picture is worth a thousand words." You can save yourself quite a few words while at the same time deepening the meaning of the change in the minds of those in your organizations through pictures.

71 Pick a Theme Song

Every army has a theme song. What's yours? The goal of this action is not to get sappy or maudlin, but to marshal energies whenever the song is played. Consider the impact of "The Marine's Hymn," "Amazing Grace," "Don't Stop Thinking About Tomorrow" and other songs that have been used to galvanize teams of individuals into armies.

The song can be useful in elevating mood, generating energy, and pulling disconnected individuals together. Pick your theme song—and play it often.

72 Develop a Cheer

Athletic teams know the value of a good cheer. A good cheer will wake up the sleeping fan, challenge the team on the field or court, and strike terror in the heart of the opponent. Your army needs a good cheer.

Ideally, the cheer should be something interesting, catchy, and something to which the team can relate—otherwise it will simply prompt confusion.

Find a cheer that will get your team going—and use it.

73 Eat

Those who have spent time in military service understand the value of meal time. During this time, friendships are built, individuals are able to "chill out," and they may engage in some planning for the future. This is also a time for the group to have fun, poke fun at each other, at the leader, the enemy, or the situation, and have a good time.

Armies eat together. The food may not be of five-star quality, but that is not the requirement. The requirement is for the team to be in one place, sharing a meal together, and connecting in that informal space.

74 Tell Stories

It is not uncommon for young Boy Scouts to tell ghost stories. These stories serve multiple purposes: they create mystery for those who are out in the wild; they challenge the scouts' creativity in coming up with stories that scare their peers; and they create a sense of "we're-all-in-this-together" for those in the woods fighting against nature.

Generating and telling stories about the group's work—what worked exceptionally well and what bombed—provides an informal way for the group to learn about its task and about those who are performing the task with them.

Stories have also long identified with the creation of "tribal memory," where those in a community have a common understanding of the past, of who they are, and of the attributes that will carry them into the future.

75 Get a Life

A significant difference between high-performing change teams and those of average performance can often be seen in the degree to which the team members live "team."

These individuals are committed to their teammates—both within the context of the activity they are working on and outside of the boundaries of that activity. They problem solve in other areas of their professional lives; they might even spend social time with each other apart from the task that brings them together.

When you see this happening, you'll know that your team has slipped into another gear—and the performance is likely to become even stronger.

76 Find a Common Enemy

This may sound like peculiar advice, but don't turn the page just yet.

If you grew up with siblings, you'll understand the example that follows. My brother and I were not particularly fond of each other. We disagreed, argued, hollered at each other and even came to blows more than once (when we were younger and less mature, of course). Yet if either of us was threatened, the other was there—no questions asked. We were blood and we stuck together.

Those whom you lead may not be blood, but they do have a common organizational or task bond that holds them together. They will likely discover that the bond becomes stronger when they realize they are fighting against an enemy that must be named, understood, and overcome. The enemy may be something as intangible as "waste," but if the enemy can be identified strategies can be developed to overcome the challenges of the enemy.

77 Fight Together

High-performing organizations or "armies," as they have been described here, need a cause. The "cause" is something that brings them together, and has them set aside differences that might, under other circumstances, destroy them.

After 9-11, America was reeling. Many were angry and confused, and all were looking to the leaders of America to help decipher this tragic situation. Out of the confusion of those historic events, one occurrence stands out: the sight of politicians from both sides of political arguments standing together singing "God Bless America."

Whether you thought the singing was wonderful, appropriate, or even wise, it is difficult to argue with the sentiment: times of great challenge call for a level of unity and commitment to our common betterment that eliminates (at least temporarily) personal agendas.

78 Breathe

This action, at first glance, may sound axiomatic, but high performing teams or armies develop a shared rhythm. That shared rhythm creates a pace, a shared stride, and a way of working that energizes the group.

Notice how a well-trained army marches together, how a skillful quarterback can find an equally-skillful receiver, or how a well trained accompanist can work with a skillful soloist.

As strange as it may sound, part of the success of these collaborations lies in the ability of the parties to create a common rhythm, to breathe, and to operate from that place of commonality.

79 Commit to Win!

There is a significant difference between winning and committing to win; you could win by an opponent simply dropping out of the race.

There are other times, however, when the win is a result of no-nonsense, no-excuse commitment to doing whatever it takes to get in the "W" column.

Does your team have a commitment to win? Are you committed to navigating the change you experience with excellence—or have you merely committed to stumbling over the finish line?

Parting thoughts...

Over-seriousness is a warning sign for mediocrity and bureaucratic thinking. People who are seriously committed to mastery and high performance are secure enough to lighten up.

– Michael Gelb

Individual commitment to a group effort—that is what makes a team work, a company work, a society work, a civilization work.

– Vince Lombardi

Chapter 6
Open Your Mouth—
Regularly

Although good communication has long been on the short list of best practices for organizational change, the organizational pressures for good communication have increased.

The reasons for this increase in required communication are many, but can be summed up by the fact that the sooner individuals understand what may be going on within the organization, the sooner they are able to "get on the bandwagon" and support or raise questions about the direction things are going. Good communication is not just a social nicety, it is an essential lubricant to effective human interaction, especially during times of change.

Current generations of employees are also less likely to accept a "we'll-get-back-to-you" response for long from their leaders. They like to be in the know, so that they are able to exert the level of influence appropriate for them.

For some, the communication task may seem to be overkill. They may feel as if all they are doing is communicating and, if that's the case, so be it. The goal is not to communicate until the boss is tired, but to communicate until the organization is able to understand and act on strategic initiatives essential to the long-term direction of the company.

80 Manage Confidentiality

Most change efforts have information that can be shared freely (it may already be commonly known) and other information that cannot be shared. All too often, however, leaders are not clear about the boundaries of sharing information.

Confidentiality is essential in any business and must be managed by the leader. As you begin any change effort, make sure you have clarified the parameters of information: what can be shared and what cannot be shared, as well as when the information can be shared.

81 Deal with Blabbermouths

Some have taken the adage "knowledge is power" and have turned it into an art form. As a result of their positions, they may have access to information that would not be available to the broader population, and they may take great delight in sharing this information inappropriately outside of the acceptable boundaries.

The premature communication of these individuals could prove devastating to persons who have not yet heard difficult information. This information could also fall into the wrong hands and present an even greater challenge; for example, it could get into the hands of the media or into the hands of competitors.

Those who are unable to manage confidential matters in a manner that reflects the weightiness of the issues at-hand must be managed in such a way that their lack of control does not create long- or short-term challenges for the organization or its employees.

82 Develop "Safe" Phrases

Employees often have access to information that would shock their leaders if it was fully known. As a result, leaders are often in a position of answering awkward questions—questions for which the timing may be inappropriate, or questions the leader cannot answer at that moment.

In situations like these, it is useful to have a set of "safe" phrases that allow the leader to respond to the question without telling more than is allowable at this stage.

In developing these phrases be sufficiently wary to not convey a "coded" message (such as when people are on "special assignment," which has come to mean "they're outta here" in many organizations).

Phrases like the following are safe and, although they may not provide the desired clarity, do answer the question:

"That hasn't been determined as of yet."

"It would be premature to offer an answer on that question."

"Many options are being considered, but nothing has been decided."

"What suggestions do you have that might work?"

83 Tell the Truth

It is not always possible to protect people and their feelings. During times of difficult organizational change, individuals inevitably want to know their status. Although you may suspect that the change will not have a happy ending, you may not be able to share this information based on many factors (i.e., possibly jeopardizing secure information, losing critical players in an untimely fashion, etc.).

You may not be able to tell all, or tell anything for that matter, but you may be able to help individuals understand the challenge of the decision, the factors that are being weighed in making a decision, and even how you may be pulling (if appropriate).

Not everything that is known has to be shared.

84 Tell YOUR Truth

One of the most powerful acts a leader can perform is to share the truth that is central to who they are. Despite the "company speak" that may be present, effective leaders may also be able to interject their own passions and commitments during times of change that can help your organization understand where you stand on an issue.

Statements that begin with "Here's what's important to me…" or "What I'm working to accomplish is…" have the potential of showing where the leader's efforts and commitments are being directed which, for many individuals, is clarifying and stabilizing.

85 Talk About What You Want

Powerful leaders are able to talk about what they want—even in the midst of a situation where they are clearly not getting what they want.

Lee Iacocca spoke about "the new Chrysler," while Jack Welch spoke about "being number 1 or number 2 in all of the industries where we operate." In both instances, these leaders were able to create an image of what they wanted, which likely both energized and challenged those who worked with them.

Avoid talking about what you don't want. This is a common mistake among leaders who are often attempting to demonstrate knowledge of the current situation in the organization—and who are attempting to issue a warning against the status quo.

Don't worry about the status quo. Talk about what you want. It will generate more energy and forward-focus than talking about what you don't want ever could.

86 Talk a Lot

This admonition may run counter to what you learned in third grade, but times of change in an organization are not times for silence. People need to hear from you, and they need to hear from you often.

Avoid the temptation for your talk to become "empty babbling;" rather, make sure that what you share has substance, relevance, and timeliness associated with it. When you come with a message, make it a message worth hearing.

87 Talk Some More

It is not uncommon to hear a leader say, "but I told them that before," as if a one-time delivery of a message is sufficient for retention and impact. It is not.

Research on communication during times of crisis suggests that it takes eight clear, concise, and consistent messages before hearers have retained the message sufficiently enough to act on it. Depressing, huh? Don't let it be.

Deliver your message in a different way, using other examples and illustrations, but arriving at the same conclusion. Make your message interesting and challenging to you and it will likely interest and challenge others.

Your message need not be "same old, same old." Your message can be fresh and captivating if you take the time to consider new ways of framing a previously heard message. The new perspective on the message may be just what some individuals in your audience need to hear in order to really get it.

88 Ask Questions

If I had a nickel for every time I've heard leaders ask questions of their audience, I would likely have ten cents. It's just not done—not nearly as often as would be useful in stimulating thinking, challenging perspectives, and in moving team members from passive roles to active roles.

The questions need not be designed to embarrass individuals, nor do they need to be pointed at a specific individual, as if they were on a quiz show. But well-honed questions delivered to an audience have a way of getting the audience to wake up, to think, and to consider the content of the message.

As long as your communication consists of you doing all the talking, exactly what would they be doing anyway? And how would you know they got anything out of your well-crafted message?

Parting thoughts...

The single biggest problem in communication is the illusion that it has taken place.

– George Bernard Shaw

To effectively communicate, we must realize that we are all different in the way we perceive the world and use this understanding as a guide to our communication with others.

– Anthony Robbins

Chapter 7
Fall in Love with Reruns

Unless you plan to retire after you read this chapter, you have probably not faced your last organizational change. Organizational changes are coming at a pace far more rapidly than any of us could imagine them coming. And, there is little evidence that they are slowing down anytime soon.

Historically, individuals were told to "hang on," to weather the change, all with the assumption that once the change occurred people could resume their previous areas of focus. Upon facing A T & T's divestiture, one employee said hopefully, "I'll be glad when this is all over, so that we can get back to business as usual." I don't know that this employee ever got her wish—and I don't know that she will.

Whether driven by technology, the environment, the economy, globalization, regulation, competition, or one of any number of other factors, change has come to stay. And those who are staying inside organizations are learning that if they are to be relevant to their employees, it is because they have developed the type of adaptability that constant change requires.

Even familiar changes (i.e., bank acquisitions) are not the same. They may seem like reruns, but each change brings with it a unique character or variation that is anything but a carbon copy of its predecessor.

But the skills that helped to develop change competence in previous efforts can be useful in future challenges as well.

89 Pack Up Your Hammock

Those who have weathered the challenges of a major change are often looking for a place to rest—somewhere where they are able to think reflective thoughts, relax a while, and enjoy the fruits of their labors.

That place no longer exists.

If you are to be relevant and valuable to your organization, it will be because you have not chosen to back off in the face of constant change. It is because you have avoided the tendency to look for a little "R and R" while on the company payroll.

Abandon such a tendency. Besides, the hammock in which you would recline has probably dry-rotted from lack of use.

90 Chop Down Your Magnolia Tree

That place of shade, where you and your compadres would recline, take it easy, and "shoot the breeze" also needs to go. You have little, if any, time to enjoy its shade and the mint juleps that would accompany your respite there.

The 21st century does not allow for lengthy times away from the "change monster" that must be fed. You don't have the time, nor the luxury of an extended period of pondering.

The next change awaits—and you must be there to meet it.

91 Let Go—Quickly

One of the challenges of rapid change is that we (and others) are often guilty of quick decisions that may have had a different outcome than we intended. Individuals may have become offended, and we, ourselves, may be suffering from ill-conceived actions associated with an organizational action.

A colleague of mine, Bill, lost his position as a result of a required downsizing within his company. His wife was seven months pregnant. The inhumanity of it all stuck with him for many years, so much so that when the individual who had to terminate him was being interviewed by the company for whom Bill worked, he refused to interview him. "There is no way I would ever consider him for anything," he fumed, even though the termination was many years earlier and was not at all personal—the individual simply had to reduce staff.

Whatever you're holding on to will likely hinder you from grabbing what you need to hold on to next.

Do what you need to do to move forward—and bring no excess baggage with you.

92 Trust

If your goal is to master change sufficiently that you become a one-man (or one-woman) change band, forget it. Change always wins, despite your best preparation.

You can, however, cultivate an attitude that keeps you on the alert for the situations in your work climate that are subject to change, and you can stay abreast of those changes that will have an impact on the work that you do.

You can develop strong, mutually-beneficial contacts with other individuals both within your company, within your industry, and in your personal life.

And beyond that, you can develop a trusting mind and a trusting heart. Ultimately, you have no final control over the outcomes of the changes that affect you, but you can set up the conditions for change in the most favorable manner.

Following that, you "trust the process."

93 Manage the Technology

Staying up-to-date on software changes, hardware changes, and the applications of technology to your work and that of your group is one of the ways you stay ahead of the change and, if you should slip slightly behind, you will be more able to catch up quickly.

This is not to suggest that you purchase the latest technological toy entering the market. It is to suggest you understand the toy, what it could conceivably do for you or for those with whom you work, and how you might utilize the toy—whether you purchase it or not.

Software magazines, websites, and professional associations are helpful means through which you can stay current with the technological changes affecting your field.

94 Smile

Maintaining a sense of humor during times of stress and change cannot be overemphasized—just ask Dilbert.

For years now, Scott Adams has used the Dilbert cartoons to offer a humorous take on the sometimes absurd changes and demands of contemporary organizations. Although Scott's work has not liberated the modern working class entirely, it has provided momentary relief from the issues that could otherwise paralyze the overly-committed.

Make time to laugh—and find the tools that will relieve the stress of your work demands through laughter. Dilbert's not a bad start.

95 Laugh a Little (or a Lot!)

According to Victor Borge, "Laughter is the closest distance between two people."

Another Victor, Victor Hugo, states, "Laughter is the sun that drives winter from the human face."

If your team has not learned to laugh—at itself, at some of the challenges it faces, at some of the absurdity of the expectations you may face—it's missing out.

Laughter is therapeutic—and should be engaged in regularly and vigorously.

96 Find a New Wrinkle

Look for the next "big deal" that will likely accompany change in your organization. Chances are it's sitting right there—out in the open—and is waiting to be discovered. Feel free to discover it.

This new wrinkle may not be a major breakthrough—it may only be another lens through which you and your team can look at change. But even if it is just that, it is a useful resource.

Look for the wrinkle. It's out there.

97 Keep Talking

For those who are extraverts (the majority of the population), thoughts become clearer when they are placed out in the open. In the mind of the extravert, this is how the thoughts become clear to him or herself, and how they are able to explore those thoughts on a deeper level. So keep talking.

Even if your conversation is to yourself, your dog or cat, or to an uninterested colleague, the act of conversation will help free your mind and open up new possible connections among the millions of bits of data that are floating around in your head.

98 Change Shoes

If you're looking for a quick way to understand change from a different perspective, change shoes. That is, walk a mile in someone else's shoes. You could accomplish this by asking questions, by shadowing him or her (i.e., following them around and observing what they do) or by changing jobs for some predetermined period of time.

Clients who have done this report a much greater and deeper appreciation for the individual in whose shoes they walked. As you face a new change, the quality of interaction between you and the other individual will likely be significantly enhanced.

99 Never Stop Recruiting

As was previously promised, you will face another change. Whether you face that change with the team you currently have, however, is not certain. What is clear is that you have the ability to influence who is on your team, and you have the ability to influence the team on which you are a member.

As you have opportunity, be on the lookout for fresh talent, fresh perspectives, and for the type of courage that will help you and your team manage the future well.

And, when you find it, grab it.

100 Pass It On

There is likely someone in your organization who would love to be in your shoes. It may be their dream, but they would not mention it to you for fear of sounding like they're hoping for your demise.

But your organization is not based on your expertise alone. It's based on having well-talented individuals in various aspects of the organization and being able to replenish the current talent with up-and-coming talent.

Help find the up-and-comers. They are the ones who will help to ensure the strength of your retirement.

Parting thoughts...

When it comes to the future, there are three kinds of people: those who let it happen, those who make it happen, and those who wonder what happened.

– John M. Richardson, Jr.

The best thing about the future is that it only comes one day at a time.

– Abraham Lincoln

I am not afraid of tomorrow, for I have seen yesterday and I love today.

– William Allen White

Postlogue:
Create a Strategic
Partnership with Technology

Probably the greatest change-related shift that has occurred in the last 100 years has been the advent and increase of technology. It is difficult to open the daily newspaper without seeing some reference to technology and the effect it is having on the way work is accomplished.

If you happened to grow up in a school where computers were not integrated into the curriculum, and if your parents did not have at least one computer in your home, changes in this arena may be particularly challenging for you.

With that thought in mind, the following actions are designed to help you overcome and navigate the particular challenges associated with technology.

101 Welcome the Presence of Technology

For many, technology is a pain in a place where they would just as soon not have a pain. For others, technology is seen as a tool—much in the same way that the telephone, automobile, or a well-sharpened pencil is.

Whatever your perspective on technology, abandoning any resistance toward it is essential. While you may be resisting technology, others (including many of your competitors) are welcoming technology and determining how it can be useful in operating their businesses more efficiently and effectively.

You should join them.

There are numerous means of getting a grip on technology. A few of those means will be discussed in the pages that follow.

102 Identify Technology Partners

There are those who absolutely love technology. They are the ones who wait for Steve Jobs' periodic introduction of Apple's latest technological wizardry, and who applaud the new toy enthusiastically.

They are also the ones who can help you use this new capability effectively in your business.

Find them. Take them to lunch. Exchange goods or services from your field of expertise for goods or services within their technology expertise.

103 Adopt an Area of Technology

There are a number of areas within the use of technology that are quite accessible, even to the most squeamish of technology users. By taking on one of these, developing your expertise there, and utilizing this area of technology, you decrease your apprehension in the use of technology and you increase the breadth of impact you can have through the use of technology.

A few areas that might not be too challenging in the beginning:

1. Write an e-mail;

2. Write a blog;

3. Develop a website;

4. Change the website;

5. Add some form of technology to your website (a questionnaire, audio or video samples).

104 Return to Action 103...

...and pick something else off the short list. Once you have completed the actions identified, new technology will be in place and you can add it to your list.

In relatively short order, you, too, may be a technology geek.